ANIMAL RELATIVES

GOLDFISH and SHARKS

FISH RELATIVES

by Dionna L. Mann

PEBBLE
a capstone imprint

Published by Pebble, an imprint of Capstone
1710 Roe Crest Drive, North Mankato, Minnesota 56003
capstonepub.com

Copyright © 2026 by Capstone. All rights reserved. No part of this publication may be reproduced in whole or in part, or stored in a retrieval system, or transmitted in any form or by any means, electronic, mechanical, photocopying, recording, or otherwise, without written permission of the publisher.

Library of Congress Cataloging-in-Publication Data
is available on the Library of Congress website.
ISBN: 9798875220401 (hardcover)
ISBN: 9798875220357 (paperback)
ISBN: 9798875220364 (ebook PDF)

Summary: Can sharks and goldfish possibly be related? Readers will explore the similarities and differences between these fish relatives in terms of life cycles, physical characteristics, skills and senses, and habitats.

Editorial Credits
Editor: Ashley Kuehl; Designer: Bobbie Nuytten; Media Researcher: Svetlana Zhurkin; Production Specialist: Whitney Schaefer

Image Credits
Alamy: Jeff Rotman, 8, WaterFrame, 10; Getty Images: Gregory S. Paulson, 17, Media Whalestock, 27, MirekKijewski, 15, Roger Tidman, 22; Shutterstock: Alessandro De Maddalena, 19, Andrea Izzotti, 9, cbpix, 14, Chaikom, 20, Chase D'animulls, cover (bottom), Chatchai chaihan, 7, chrisbrignell, 11, Daria Rosen (background), cover, 1, 30, dien, 4, Fiona Ayerst, 21, frantisekhojdysz, 13, freedomnaruk, 18, Helen E. Grose, 29, Jennifer Mellon Photos, 28, Jonas Gruhlke, 23, kaschibo, 5, Lotus_studio, cover (top), MP cz, 26, Rabbitmindphoto, 24, Sergey Uryadnikov, 25, Sergii Kumer, 12, Sukpaiboonwat, 16

Any additional websites and resources referenced in this book are not maintained, authorized, or sponsored by Capstone. All product and company names are trademarks™ or registered® trademarks of their respective holders.

Printed and bound in China. PO 006276

TABLE OF CONTENTS

No Kidding, We're Kin! 4

Growing Up.. 6

Underwater Bodies 12

Making Their Move...................................18

Time to Dine 24

Predator or Prey....................................... 28

Can You Remember?..................................30

Animal Jokes 30

Glossary 31

Index..32

About the Author.....................................32

Words in **bold** are in the glossary.

NO KIDDING, WE'RE KIN!

Is it true? A cute little goldfish is **kin** to a shark? It's true, all right! Sharks and goldfish are both fish.

They share many features. They both have fins to help them swim. They have gills that help them breathe. But they have lots of differences too. Let's take a look!

GROWING UP

Goldfish and sharks both start life small. A female goldfish lays hundreds or thousands of eggs. Then a male goldfish **fertilizes** some of them.

Baby goldfish grow in their eggs for two to seven days. Then they hatch. A baby goldfish is called a fry. But not many goldfish eggs become fry. Adult goldfish eat most of them!

For most sharks, babies grow inside their mother's body. She gives birth to a live baby shark, or pup. Other shark mothers lay eggs. The babies grow in egg cases outside their mother's body.

a pygmy shark pup

FUN FACT

An egg sac outside the mother shark's body is called a mermaid's purse.

Some sharks have only two pups at a time. Others have more than 100!

Shark pups can take care of themselves as soon as they're born. They can eat, swim, and protect themselves. Goldfish fry can also survive on their own after they hatch.

Sharks have a longer life than goldfish. Most live 20 to 30 years. Greenland sharks can live 270 years! Most goldfish live 10 to 15 years. But some **species** live longer.

UNDERWATER BODIES

Both sharks and goldfish live in water. Goldfish live in fresh water. Some live in ponds. Others live in bowls or tanks in people's homes.

Most shark species need salt water to live. They live in oceans around the world.

Goldfish and sharks have body parts that help them live underwater. Both animals have gills near their heads to help them breathe. Water moves through the gills. The gills take oxygen from the water.

Sharks and goldfish both have good eyesight. Sharks can see well even in dark, cloudy water. Goldfish can see things 15 feet (4.6 meters) away.

Sharks and goldfish both have scales on their skin. The scales protect them as they swim.

shark scales

Shark scales are super strong. They're shaped like teeth. Goldfish scales are rounder. They look like half-moons. They are not as strong as shark scales.

MAKING THEIR MOVE

Sharks and goldfish use their fins to move. They swim up. They dive down. They go in circles. They can zip forward. They can even jump out of the water.

But sharks swim much faster than goldfish. The shortfin mako shark can swim 31 miles (50 kilometers) per hour!

Both fish have body parts that help them float. Goldfish have a swim **bladder**. It fills with air. They can use it to go up or down. Sharks do not have a swim bladder. But they do have a fatty **liver**. It helps them float.

FUN FACT

Some sharks suck in air to help them float. They let some of it out to go deeper.

One big difference is inside their bodies. Goldfish have bones. Their backbones and ribs are made of bone.

Sharks do not have bones. Instead, sharks have cartilage. This firm tissue is softer than bone. It bends more. It also weighs less than bone.

TIME TO DINE

Goldfish are omnivores. They eat both plants and animals. Pet goldfish may eat bits of vegetables or fruit. Wild goldfish eat plants and insect **larvae**.

Most sharks eat only meat and fish. That can include many different ocean animals. But some kinds of sharks eat meat and seagrass. Those sharks are omnivores like their goldfish cousins.

Sharks use their teeth to tear and chomp their food. Did you know that goldfish also have teeth? Goldfish teeth are in the back of their throat. They use them to grind their food.

Both sharks and goldfish are powerful sniffers. They use their sense of smell to find food.

FUN FACT

Unlike sharks, goldfish do not have stomachs.

PREDATOR OR PREY

Sharks are top **predators**. They are powerful hunters. Few animals will try to eat a shark. But some smaller sharks are not safe. Bigger sharks may eat them!

Goldfish in the wild are often **prey**. Lots of animals eat goldfish. Birds and raccoons are the most dangerous predators. But other animals may eat them too.

CAN YOU REMEMBER?

1. What body part do sharks and goldfish use to breathe?
2. What do sharks and goldfish eat?
3. What do scales do?
4. What is a baby goldfish called?
5. True or false: Sharks have bones in their bodies.

Check your answers at the bottom of page 31!

ANIMAL JOKES

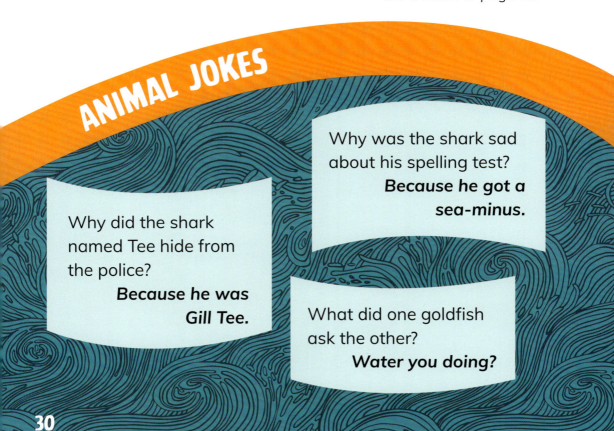

Why was the shark sad about his spelling test? **Because he got a sea-minus.**

Why did the shark named Tee hide from the police? **Because he was Gill Tee.**

What did one goldfish ask the other? **Water you doing?**

GLOSSARY

bladder (BLAD-ur)—a body organ that holds liquid or gas

fertilize (FUR-tuh-lize)—to start the process of producing babies

kin (KIN)—related animals or people

larvae (LAHR-vee)—animals at the stage of growth right after they hatch

liver (LIV-ur)—a body organ that helps keep blood clean

predator (PRED-uh-tur)—an animal that hunts, kills, and eats other animals

prey (PRAY)—an animal that is hunted to be eaten by another animal

species (SPEE-sheez)—a group of the same kind of animal; members of the same species can mate and have young

1. Gills; 2. Both eat meat; goldfish eat plants too; 3. Protect goldfish and sharks as they swim; 4. A fry; 5. False

INDEX

babies, 6, 8–10
bones, 22–23

cartilage, 23

eating, 6, 10, 24–26, 28–29
eggs, 6, 8–9
eyesight, 15

fins, 5, 18
floating, 20–21
fresh water, 12
fry, 6, 10

gills, 5, 14

lifespan, 11

protection, 10, 16
pups, 8–10

salt water, 13
scales, 16–17
smell, 27
speed, 19
swimming, 5, 10, 18–20

teeth, 26

ABOUT THE AUTHOR

Dionna L. Mann is a children's book author who spent nearly 25 years working and volunteering in her local school system. As an independent researcher, she especially enjoys discovering lesser-known individuals shining in the margins of African American history. Dionna's debut novel for young readers, *Mama's Chicken & Dumplings* (Margaret Ferguson Books, 2024) was chosen as a Junior Library Guild Gold Selection. Find Dionna online at dionnalmann.com.